Dear Life, Here I Am.
Sincerely, Andrea Lynn Samuels

A collection of prose, art and a personal story of inspiration

Dear Tozella & Terry,

Thank you so much for your warmth. It is a pleasure to meet both of you. May God continue to bless and keep you.

Love,
Andrea L. Samuels

Dear Life, Here I Am.

Sincerely, Andrea Lynn Samuels

by

Andrea Lynn Samuels

DORRANCE
PUBLISHING CO
EST. 1920
PITTSBURGH, PENNSYLVANIA 15222

Dorrance Publishing Co
585 Alpha Drive
Suite 103
Pittsburgh, PA 15238
Visit our website at *www.dorrancebookstore.com*

ISBN: 978-1-4809-0556-6
eISBN: 978-1-4809-0573-3

Introduction

Thank you, Lord, for blessing me with the ability to verbally express feelings and life as I see it. Thank you, Lord, for placing in my life people who have helped me find the courage to share with others.

I first discovered my thirst for the arts as a small child through the exposure that my mom and dad gave me, and realized I had genetically received some of the same artistic gifts that both of my parents had through numerous "shows" that I developed and executed for them in the living room of our apartment, which included a combination of singing, dancing, dramatic interpretations/acting (smile) drawing, painting, reading stories, and reciting poetry. In 1973 at the age of four, my parents enrolled me in the Harlem School of the Arts, where I took ballet, African/ethnic dance, and voice lessons. Growing up in New York City gave me the opportunity to have unlimited indulgence in the arts, to add to my formal training in that wonderful world, which I happily soaked up and craved, further opening up my heart, mind, understanding, and acceptance that I was an artist.

While in the eighth grade at St. Matthew Lutheran School in Manhattan, we had a writing assignment to create a book of poetry. It was love at first write! I was hooked on expressing myself. Since that time, circa 1982/83, I had secretly been writing poetry, putting fire, love, hurt, indifference, retrospect, and reverence on paper.

Being somewhat "exposed," while in an honors English class at A. Philip Randolph Campus High School in New York City, the poem that I wrote for an assignment was published in the 1984 *Cougars' Lair*, my high school's literary publication. That would be "The Great Door of Time." In that publication under the chapter of *Solitude*, my poem was the last poem printed, to close the book. I have chosen to do the same in mine.

Mom, what can I say? Through God, you gave me life. There are really no words except you are my rock and I love you. Thank you for loving me from the time I cried constantly from colic as an infant, to a flippant-mouthed youth, with hair colors that the most brilliant rainbow would envy, to an adult who was once married and is the mother of a very bright and tenacious son, who you say reminds you of me in so many ways.

Etu Evans, down through the years, you have been that baseline in my life, steadily encouraging me to realize my dreams, always giving me the right push and positive reinforcement precisely at the time that I need to hear it, without notice. What a marvelous, living example you have been to me. I love you. Thank you.

Dr. Danielle Edwards, thank you, my dear friend, for being that person to reignite that artistic flame again in my dad when he painted "The Garden of Eden," after thirty-some odd years of remaining dormant, giving him a new excitement, which I believe added some time to his life, and for reading and listening to some of my work.

My friend, Paul Williams III, thank you for beautifully capturing my dad's work through your lens, helping to bring his paintings to life in my book.

Jackie Wallace, thank you for believing in my dad's pieces and contacting your friend, art gallery owner Ed Harris. Ed, thank you for taking the time to look at my dad's work and graciously planning to host his art show. I love all of you dearly.

Zandrea Blodgette and Janie Diggs: Like Danielle, you understand all too well the tumultuous journey that cancer takes you on with your fathers, who fought the battle against cancer, too. Infinite gratitude to both of you for your understanding, sisterhood, and unconditional support throughout my plight. Love always.

Sherry Waters, thank you for your faith in me and connecting with my story and covering it years ago in your publication, when I first birthed the idea of publishing a book to honor my dad's life.

To author and friend Helen Kimbrough and Attorney Nichelle A. Levy, you have continued to pull the thread through the needle of my life's garment to finish it. Your gentle encouragement and faith over the years in me has no price that I can apply. I gratefully thank you.

Tewanna Brazzley, thank you for your support and walking this journey with me for my book not only as my friend, but business manager, and for your understanding of my passion around fighting cancer.

To my awesome and talented cousin, Rodney K. Gary, thank you for your photography and creativity, capturing what I wanted to convey for the cover of my book, some of the photography right inside of the book and my website. You brought to life, my vision beautifully.

To my late great dad, writer, poet and artist, Calvin Henry Samuels: I still feel your love surrounding me even after your passing. You courageously fought cancer for seven years that we know of, and you grew tired and took your rest peacefully on Monday, July 21, 2008. You painted beautiful works of art while battling cancer and I am honored to be able to share some of those pieces with others in this book.

Seeing my dad so happy and alive and painting with a purpose through his continuous fatigue inspired me to want to share my poetry with others. And Dad, once I shared with you that I had been writing poetry, like Mom, you encouraged and supported me to keep writing. Thank you. I am so glad that you had the chance to hear me read my tribute to you, "Riverside Drive." Thank you for that slow, simple walk, Dad, down Riverside Drive. My love and admiration for you is forever.

The above are some of the major pieces which helped to complete this part of the puzzle of my life's story. I am honored that you have chosen to take the time to walk down some of the sidewalks and streets that I have traveled, sharing some conversations that I have had with others, as well as some of my own feelings, thoughts, and experiences.

Dare to tell your story and be that warm blanket and bowl of hot, home-made chicken soup in the dead of winter, or a tall glass of ice water on a steamy summer day, either warming and soothing someone's soul, or cooling someone down. Let them have an opportunity to relate their story to yours by sharing your artistic gift, an extension of you.

More Gratitude and Love

During our lives, we all are going to face some type of adversity, and we cannot go through these times alone. My mother and I have been blessed to have in our lives an incredible army of angels who have been with us to celebrate the victories that my dad experienced, and remained solid rocks as we were in very dark and uncertain places as he battled cancer, and to comfort us after our great loss. I do not see any other appropriate way to immortalize my gratitude for these amazing individuals other than to ink their names for all to see.

Whether it was prayer in the midnight hour, words of encouragement and love, a visit with Dad to give Mom relief while she ran an errand, picking up items for my mom, a light-hearted meal with friends old and new, a treat to a pampering experience, an outlet to relieve stress through exercise, help with my son's childcare while visiting my dad in New York, an ear, a shoulder, a hand, a hug, and countless other ways.

Our angels, listed from the heart: Charles, the late Earl and Martha, Josephine, Frances and the entire Gary family, Bessie Wheeler, Leronda Butler, Rev. Marian E. Samuels Grier, Sandra Mayo Jackson, the Samuels and Mayo families, Sean Williams and the Williams family, Daisy and Johnnie Ellis, Calvin, Barbara and Tosha Hudson, Deacon Catherine Coleman, Dr. Thelma Smith, Deborah McKenzie, Sequetta Blackmon, Danielle and Sheldon Edwards, Zandrea Blodgette, Janie Diggs, Etu Evans, Lisa Walker, Toni Rivers, Stacey Wallace, Tewanna Sanders Brazzley, Susi Laub, Wendy and Andrew Phillips, Maria and Finian Curran, Skeeter Holly, Kristie Huntley, the Johnson Family: Rev. Johnson, Phyllis and Ravi, Christina and Marlon Williams, Paul Williams III, Jackie Wallace, Tonia, Shean and the Lewis family, Rev. Barbara Thomas, Carolyn Fraiser, Barbara Butler, Betty and Larry Mackey, Tammy Greene—The Jazz Diva, Bill Newnan, Jeremi Snook, formerly of the Uptown Shelter and the Uptown Shelter team, Nettie Reeves of N'Shape with N, LLC, Candace Petty-Parker, Shannon and late Third

Jamison, Nicole and Jonathan Perry, Cathy Albert, Bob Fleming, the McKay family, the late Adele Walker, Dr. Andrew Evans and the team at St. Luke's Roosevelt Hospital, Hospice of New York City, the 640-644 Riverside Drive Tenants Association, Rev. Alistair Drummond and the West End Presbyterian Church family in New York, New York, The Convent Avenue Baptist Church family in New York, New York, the Friendship Missionary Baptist Church family in Charlotte, North Carolina, Alexander Henry and the team at Einstein Bagels in Charlotte, North Carolina, Guy Kemp, the St. Matthew Lutheran School Class of 1983: Tess Gladden, Anuk Goodwin Stewart, Felicia Gray, Patrick Greenaway, Tisha Fraiser, Clement Schulze, Michael Paul Jackson, Zach Mabry, John Waller, Rory Eason Douthard, Nicole Penn, Karyn Davis, Dana Wilkinson Lynch and Deana Linton, Erica Eaton, Mr. Kaufman and the Hardware Specialty Team-Long Island City, New York, and the Coler-Goldwater Memorial Hospital Team-FDR Island, New York.

Yes, there are angels on earth who will help us fly when our bodies and souls are weary.

Thank you dearly for helping us to fly when we could not do it by ourselves.

We love you and shall never forget what you have done for us.

Finding Purpose in the Pain

"The private side of defining our personal mark is often laced in pain. It is the downside, the unexpected side that gives the blueprint life. This pain can often become passion for a better way, a change of direction, hope and inspiration."
—Melissa Dawn Johnson-Simkins, *Lifestyle* brand strategist and Velvet Suite Marketing Consulting Group, author of *Brand Me, Make Your Mark*

"Dad, I think there may be some type of imbalance in your body because your toenail is badly withered," I remember saying to him sometime during the summer of 2000 while giving him a pedicure. At that time, I operated my own nail business as a licensed nail technician in Charlotte, North Carolina, and my parents were down visiting me from New York City as we were heading to my dad's family reunion in Marianna, Florida. "Oh, it's nothing. I just probably need some type of topical agent to clear it up," he said. Although I insisted otherwise, he did not budge.

Fast forward to March 2001. I remember as if it were last Sunday afternoon when I received the call from my mom stating that my dad had been diagnosed with colon cancer. Yes. She had said the big "C." My world immediately was changed. I cried. I could not breathe. All was still. At that time, my husband told me just get home and do not worry about anything in Charlotte, that he had everything covered.

Upon my arrival in New York, I was so proud to be there to support my mom, strong and determined Andrea to the rescue! (smile). While at the hospital as my dad was being prepped for surgery to remove the colon cancer, the next thing I knew, I felt faint and woozy and I just wanted to sit down on the cool hospital floor for just a little while. Trying to find a vein for the nurse to insert a needle was a little bit too much for me to watch. While on his back, my dad smiled and teased me, ordering me to go to the waiting room! The invasive colon surgery, performed at St. Luke's Roosevelt Hospital in Manhattan, was a huge success, finishing about an hour and a half earlier than had been anticipated.

Quickly turning the pages again, we are now in 2005. My mom was already in the Carolinas visiting with family as she was now a retiree and her time was now her own, and my dad drove down from New York to join us as both sets of grandparents were accompanying my husband and me to take our young son, Sean II, who was three at that time, to see Thomas The Tank Engine in the Great Smokey Mountains that July. My dad happily came down, as there was nothing that he would not do for his only grandson, "the little guy" as he often called him.

Immediately, I witnessed firsthand the hacking cough that my mom told me about and stayed on my dad to get checked out. Knowing how invincible my dad felt with a "Supermanish" mentality, as he was always there for others in time of sickness and need, I knew his visit to Charlotte would not be the forum to scold him to go to see his primary care physician (PCP) because he would brush it off as an allergy as he continued to do with my mom. So, I left him a strong and direct voicemail on my parents' landline in New York so it would be there to greet him upon his return to the city.

Thankfully, that worked. He went to see his PCP for a checkup, who took X-rays, evaluated them, and told my dad that he did not like what he saw and immediately referred him to a radiation oncologist. The thorough team of physicians—Dr. Michael Grossbard, Dr. Douglas S. Cohen, and Dr. Andrew Evans—at St. Luke's Roosevelt Hospital gave my dad an MRI not only of the area of concern of his primary care physician, which was the lung area, but also of his brain.

My mom got the grim diagnosis from Dad: the cancer had metastasized to his lungs and brain. Brain, operable; lungs, inoperable, because the cancer was wrapped around his ribs. My mom immediately packed up what she could and shipped the rest of her items home and headed back to New York City, to be with my dad as he attacked this returning beast once again.

We celebrated a very successful invasive brain surgery to remove the cancer the week before Thanksgiving 2005, performed at St. Luke's Roosevelt Hospital in New York City. To our amazement, "Grandpa" felt great after surgery and would not have it any other way than to join us to take his grandson to see Santa at Macy's Herald Square! Wow. So with his "boo-boo," as Sean II called grandpa's surgical wound, we had a magical time at Santaland, a priceless memory for all of us to hold on to and to cherish.

Next came aggressive chemotherapy and radiation, as well as two successful stereotactic radiosurgeries. Through all of his medical treatment and battle with cancer, he would not retire and he never complained, but instead, painted beautiful works of art, inspired by a very dear friend of mine.

In 2004, while visiting with me at my home in Charlotte, North Carolina, Danielle Edwards looked a bit closer at a painting she had seen on my kitchen wall numerous times. "Is that C. H. Samuels I see in the corner of that painting?" she asked. "Yes, it is," I said. "He must paint something for me," Danielle stated. Thus, "A Melody to Shirley Bassey" was the spark of the creation of many beautiful paintings created by my dad. Danielle's piece, which Dad entitled "In the Garden of Eden," was my dad's artistic rebirth, the first piece that he painted after about thirty years of dormancy. My mom and I had begged him to paint again for years and he did not. Not until *he* was ready.

Another dear friend of mine, Jacqueline Wallace, saw some of my dad's paintings and said that she must introduce him to friend and gallery owner, Ed Harris. He and Ed met and talked and dad beamed as he and Ed discussed him hosting an art show for my dad, at his gallery in Charlotte, North Carolina, sometime in 2005. My dad sketched and painted feverishly as he prepared for his art show until his hand would not go anymore. He continued to fight the cancer and laughed at himself while doing so, making my mom and I laugh right along with him. This helped us as my mom and I had some very frustrating and dark moments, especially during some of Dad's more difficult days. Some of those moments were shared and other moments individually in each of our quiet spaces.

In May of 2008, as I shared some of my poetry with my mom and dad, including a tribute to him entitled "Riverside Drive," he told me to "keep writing."

My dad was bedridden for only the last three weeks of his life, as hospice was brought in, providing wonderful support to my mom as his primary caregiver, and to me during my last visit with him. My mom had called to tell me, "I think you need to come home now." I immediately booked a flight home and went to New York, to be with Dad and Mom.

As many times as I felt the excitement of arriving home and of seeing the New York City skyline on the approach to LaGuardia, this time, it was not the same, for I had feelings without a reasonable doubt that as the plane smoothly landed in The Big Apple, that was the last time that I would see my dad alive.

On Sunday, July 13, 2008, after my weeklong visit as I was preparing to head back to Charlotte, North Carolina, I repeatedly asked my mom if she needed me to stay until Uncle Charles arrived from Columbia, South Carolina the next day so she would not be alone. She insisted that she was okay, and that she would be fine until her brother arrived as he purchased a one-way ticket and would be with her as long as she needed him. As God would have it, while we were having dinner, I received a call from the airline that my flight was canceled and the next flight out would be Monday. In all of my many years of flying, I have never received a call from an airline that my flight was canceled. Delayed, yes, canceled, no. Therefore, my mom was never alone during the last two weeks of my dad's life.

Before I left Charlotte, I had a very candid, powerful, and timely conversation with another one of my good friends, Zandrea Blodgette. Zandrea knew this journey all too well, as she lost her father to cancer several years prior. She said, "Drea, if you can, when you are ready and in your dad's presence, pray with him and let him know that you and your mom will be okay. A lot of times, our loved ones hold on for us." When I first arrived around midnight because my flight was delayed leaving Charlotte, even though it was late, I directly went and sat in the room with my dad. He felt my presence, opened his eyes, and smiled at me. I felt so warm and wonderful. I told him that I loved him very much and he whispered back that he loved me, too. I knew my dad was very tired and I also knew how much he loved my mom and me. He was our protector. We were his "big sugar" and "little sugar"—"The Samuels Three." It was hard, hard for all of us. A few days into my visit, I felt so strong and I prayed that prayer that Zandrea talked to me about, the three of us—"The Samuels Three"—holding hands. It was a very peaceful place for us.

Months later after my dad's passing, my mom told me, "You have to carry the torch." I knew that I had to follow through with the book. At that time, I thought long and hard about how I could honor him and keep his memory alive. Thus, I have weaved some of his art into my book.

The support, love, and encouragement that I have received from both of my parents and my dad's artistic legacy, blended with God's divine plan, have continued to push me to finish this book, even when I was hesitant. Still not sure to follow through with publishing this book, came Tuesday, March 24, 2009....

In the first year after my dad's passing, significant holidays and specific dates were sometimes difficult to navigate. As I write these words, my dad's birthday, June 3, and Father's Day 2009, have not yet arrived.

My heart was very heavy as March 24 approached, because every day, I see a happy and fun picture of my dad, my son, me, and Geoffrey the Giraffe at Toys R Us at Times Square in New York City, taken on March 24, 2008, hanging on the wall in my son's room. About a month or so prior to March 24, 2009, I received an invitation to two wonderful events in Atlanta, Georgia, from my good friend, Etu Evans, celebrity shoe designer and president of Solesville-The Etu Evans Foundation: one to an inaugural women's retreat, organized and hosted by Melissa Dawn Johnson on Saturday, March 21, 2009 and the other event, a fundraising dinner for his foundation that Etu was having at Café Circa. Etu's event was on March 24. I checked my calendar and immediately saw that I would be able to make Etu's event. I was so excited and happy for him and looked forward to the trip with much anticipation. In the meantime, there had been some health concerns with one of my uncles and my mom was keeping me informed as the family received more information. I told her to call me whenever she found something out, that I wanted to know as soon as she does. So, on the morning of March 24, as I was excitedly preparing to leave for Atlanta, she reluctantly called me, stating she did not want to put a damper on my trip, but I reassured her that was okay, that I wanted to know: her brother, my godfather/Uncle Earl, had been diagnosed with multiple myeloma cancer. So, with a very excited but heavy heart, I drove to Atlanta to support my good friend.

As I grabbed the handle to Café Circa's door—arriving promptly in my usual fashion at 6:00 pm—as I entered the restaurant, I took a deep breath and said to myself, "This is going to be a fabulous evening!" I had no idea how profound that statement would be as I had no clue that the beautiful sisters and people I would meet would be the final stitches to complete my custommade garment cut from my pattern that I designed, the final edit for my book. Upon greeting me in his usual promptness and intuitiveness, Etu said, "Andrea! Glad that you could make it! Are you okay?"

I told Etu that I was glad to be there to support him and that I was fine, stating that I was starving and needed to immediately get a table so I could dig in. (Anyone who knows me knows that this would be a true statement, and at almost any given time, I can eat portions of food designed for a man.)

Knowing me all too well, Etu could see that there was something wrong with me, but I was not going to share the personal significance that March 24 was to me, not at that time. That was his night. I was not going have him babysitting me for the entire evening, because of his concern, making sure that I was okay. I would tell him at another time.

As the evening went on, the following sisters are some of the most beautiful and inspiring women that I have met all at once, some of whom are published, successful business owners, and understanding firsthand what it means to experience and overcome insurmountable challenges, coming through them with grace. They showed me nothing but pure love and support of my upcoming book: Andrea, Annette Whitlock, Elizabeth Williams, Yolanda Seals, Angela Fletcher, Beth Borden-Goodman, Dr. Kordie Green, Angilla Jones, Kizmet Mills, and Melissa Dawn Johnson. As I conversed with these powerful women, I began to realize that the timing of Etu's event was no accident, but it was God ordering my steps. Melissa shared with me that she prays as she is about to embark on a meeting or a conference, asking God to order her steps. "This is really *your* night, Drea," Etu said to me during the event. All I could say was, "Wow!"

I would come to find a few months later after I read Melissa's powerful book that each of us really are the holders of the key to our own success. I, too, ask God to order my steps, as I did on my way to Atlanta that day. Melissa said that "I must do this," referring to following through with the book and she handed me her card. She also stated, "You have no excuse now not to do this."

I had been struggling for many months about typing this part of the book, as it was very painful for me to bring to life, through written form, the journey. However, I have found it to be very therapeutic and healing, something that I had to do because in doing so, sharing my story can encourage others, and that's the key, helping others by sharing a part of us, a part of our story, a part of our journey. That evening at Café Circa changed my life....

The author with Etu Evans
Tuesday, March 24, 2009
Café Circa-Atlanta, Georgia

"All dreams manifest from the magic of belief. Fear is not a death sentence, but is often the funeral that buries most who lurk in the dark shadows of those with the illuminated faith to seize the moment."
  —Etu Evans, celebrity shoe designer and president of Solesville-The Etu Evans Foundation

Dedication

To humankind: Live.

Mom, thank you for your continued, unconditional love and support.

Godfather and Uncle Earl, we knew that you were tired. Thank you for understanding the powerful gift of time and being a part of so many imprints in my heart and my mind. May you rest in peace.

Earl Gary: September 8, 1941 – September 3, 2009

Dad, thank you for leaving a powerful legacy behind for me to use as my life's blueprint.

We know that you are resting peacefully with God.

Calvin H. Samuels: June 3, 1933 – July 21, 2008

Contents

Listing of Paintings, Photos, and Acknowledgments

Cover, front inside and back inside photographs taken by Rodney K. Gary, Photographer and Owner, OneMomentOneShot Photography, Savannah, Georgia taken at Forsyth Park, Savannah, Georgia

Paintings by Calvin H. Samuels:

> "In the Garden of Eden," Mr. and Mrs. Sheldon Edwards, owners. Used with written permission.
> "Nightingale of Chaplin Drive"
> "Dance of the Maidens"
> "A Melody to Shirley Bassey"
> "Sheba Arrives in Jerusalem"
> "An Exercise in Blue"
> "Dawn Comes to Darfur"

Photos:

> Photos of paintings taken by Paul Williams, III of Paul3 Photography, Charlotte, North Carolina
> About the Author photo taken by Elizabeth Benfield
> *Calvin* and Lottie Samuels, 1965
> *Storm Clouds* taken by the author
> *Ducks at the Lake*, Charlotte, North Carolina. Taken by the author.
> 141st Street *and* Riverside Drive street sign, taken by the author and *Riverside Drive* profile of author, taken by Lottie G. Samuels
> Andrea as a junior at A. Philip Randolph Campus High School in 1986
> Father and daughter 1973, taken by Lottie G. Samuels

The Legacy

After her dad's passing, Andrea's mother discovered many writings they did not know anything about that her father had tucked away.

Reading through his work has been so soothing for Andrea, and she feels even more connected to her dad, as she sees on paper, through God, she has inherited the gift from her father to pen random words and thoughts, connecting them to translate into poetic expression.

On the next page is an excerpt from one of her father's many writings, entitled "The Land," along with the artistic rebirth sparked by her friend, Danielle Edwards, "In the Garden of Eden."

One generation passeth away, and another generation cometh; but the earth abideth for ever. Ecclesiastes 1:4, KJV

The Land
by the late Calvin H. Samuels

Time and again I have tried to arrange for a sunrise as spectacular and as beautiful as the ones I witnessed upon my inception, as a world for the benefit and aesthetic appreciation of man and beast. But, somehow, I cannot. The divine beauty remains, but something, some quality beyond explanation is lost. In those glorious days, the sun would burst over the horizon, permeating the clouds and early morning haze like a huge ball of orange dye cast into a pool of water. Swiftly and gently, I was bathed in its invisible rays of warmth....

Chapter One
God

Something…
…Unequalled.

You know what it is, think!
Say no words, my friend.
Just sense it.

Capture it!
Feel it!
See it!

Nature.

May

Like mid-fall, rather subtle weather reminds us,
Spring has arrived.

A cool breeze revives everything in its path.
Delicate teardrops from heaven splatter against the earth's floor,
Once again, reminding us,
Reminding us April is here.

The rain quenches the earth's thirst.
Flowers start to bloom.
May.

The Poetry of God

One could just breathe a breath of fresh air
And sense the purity of what God has done.
Row after row as I walk through the park,
There are various trees,
And none are alike.
No, not one.

Clouds in the sky like cotton,
White, fluffy, metamorphic.

Sometimes, the rhythm of the rain drums up a soothing beat.
Much appreciated when one is relaxing, when one is asleep.

The melody the sunshine carries livens up someone's dismal day.
The stars wink in the night.
Oh, one mustn't forget the sea's never endless flow.
Where does it start, end, I don't know.

Amazing, though complex to grasp.
But, if one reads the poetry of God,
One will see, one will know,
He is sovereign over all of the land.

God Is Near

When you take your first glimpse of the morning sun,
you'll know that a new day has begun.
And,
when you step outside and take in the beautiful free air,
you will understand how the trees, flowers, and other forms of nature can
survive.

It's also nice to know,
coming home in the evening, you may have the privilege of walking by an
untouched area of nature, seeing it in its purest form.

And, the breathtaking sight of the sunset,
reflected on a placid stream.

You can now also look and then see in the east, the night starts to take over,
pushing the sun farther and farther into the west.

As you now lay down to sleep for the night, you can smile and say to yourself,
"God is near."

Fall Morning, Thank You Lord

I look up at the clear blue sky,
I look around at the birds soaring high,
I see the trees bending to the command of the wind,
The crisp wind on my face.
I can't see it, but I know it's there.

I see the rich colors of fall leaves on the trees,
Some falling as I enjoy the scenery.
Nature's eye candy to behold.

I listen to the ripple of the creek,
I look at the tall oak trees, roots so deep,
And I am frozen by the awesome wonder that I see,
My God, my Creator has given to me.

To see His wonder.
To taste the many fruits of the earth.
To cherish this day I have been given.
To love the skin that I am living in.

I thank you Lord for your gifts of unmatched beauty.
And I thank you Lord that I am able to see,
Another beautiful fall morning.

And So I Pray

So many changes in life.
So much going on all around us.

I feel like a stranger in my own land.
Don't recognize the landscape of the terrain anymore,
for it has changed so.
Feel guilty sometimes for being happy when so many people are hurting and
are dismayed.
And so at times, I suppress how I really feel out of quiet respect and empathy
for their struggles.

Life is so different now,
not the same as it used to be, and it's hard.
It's hard when you don't have people and things familiar around you any-
more.
Emotions raw like exposed wire, kept quiet though.
Don't want to disturb anyone else's pain with my burdens.

I don't know what I would do,
if I did not have God to turn to,
to hear his soft whisper, soothing my soul, telling me it's going to be okay.
And so I pray.

Chapter Two

JoyPainLovePassion

A rebellious sort of feeling.
It's pushing you, pushing you to your last nerve.
Boom! Pow!
It sends helplessness across your body.
Boggles the system.
Comes at you like fire.
Laughs at you deceitfully.
Alarm!

You're cooling down now.
Gracefully.
Daintily.
Quietly,
Like a swan gliding on water,
A spectacle.
Ahhhhh....

Nightingale of Chaplin Drive

Happy

I can't contain myself!
Oh, oh, my gosh!
I could scream!
Can't stop jumping around!

Why?

Because, you said hi to me.

"I Do"

Do you have any idea how you have changed my life?
Sometimes, I feel like a flower,
Opening up beneath the golden warmth of your love,
Responding to the sunshine that the very sight of you brings me.
That is how I feel when I am with you.

It's a wonderful feeling made all the more special,
Because I know this is just the beginning,
Of the understanding and trust that we will share.

For with time, I want to know you completely.
I want to give all of myself to you, holding nothing back.
Except for the mystery that allows us to be two separate persons,
We will be joined by one beautiful love.

Happy Anniversary

I sit and I ponder,
Trying to remember the very instant I saw you.
With time, clarity gives way to fuzzy snippets of memories.

It was a long, long time ago,
When I happened on that café on Fifth and Main.
Do you remember?
What in the world was I doing there anyway?
Strange, strange how God guides our feet to our destiny.

I can't really recall how we even began to speak.
But I do remember how my heart fluttered,
Because it still does.

I also remember how pure you smelled,
Because you still do.

I am also very clear on the taste of your sweet breath,
Because it still is, sweet.

Then, I still remember the twinkle in those soulful eyes,
Beaming as bright as stars on a clear evening.
Because they are still saying "I love you,"
The same way they did all of those many, many years ago.

I loved you then,
I love you now,
I'll love you forever, until death do us part.

Happy anniversary, my love.

Reassured

Picture a calm, serene lake just before dusk.
You and I are standing at its banks,
watching, waiting for the sun's departure.

Pulling me close, you whisper nothing, but I know you care, love.
We are each separate in our endeavors, dreams,
But together, we share closeness in our feelings.

We start to get a little cautious because of the mystery the darkness has created,
now that the sun has gone down.

This darkness reminds us of the raging tides of life we have experienced,
And this makes us uneasy, restless.

But, like a candle, when we kiss, our light shines brightly,
And burns on through the darkness of the night.
Now we know that we'll last forever,
Because now, we are reassured.

An Evening Stroll

By chance, we stopped by the same park, at the same time,
and you were walking down by the south end of the lake,
which is my favorite part.

As the evening sun met the water,
hues of yellow, orange, lavender, and deep pink,
gave your skin a perfect glow,
which will forever remain frozen in my mind.

As we moved closer,
your eyes made me feel as though I were crisp air,
blowing against your smooth skin to refresh you.

When you touched me,
I felt my blood turn to fire as it moved through my veins to sustain me.
And when my knees buckled, you gently caught me in your strong arms so I
wouldn't fall,
and then you lowered me to the cool evening ground.
When your soft lips met mine,
I felt as though I were the first star seen in the sky on a clear evening.

Time passed so quickly and as dusk made its way for night,
we knew that we must go.
By the way, what is your name and will I ever see you again?

Masterpiece

My heart stopped beating.
I was frozen because I was in awe of every inch of your perfectness,
like you were carefully carved by a sculptor's steady, definitive hand,
created for the world to admire.

As I studied your eyes deeply,
I saw your interpretation of life in ways that I have never considered,
and I wanted to understand you more.

When I looked at your soft lips, I could feel them meet mine
with such compassion and ownership,
but ever so tenderly and with such care.

Your skin was like the finest of fabrics from the Far East,
and I wanted to wrap myself in it,
and feel your luxuriousness.
I likened your fingers to the limbs of an old oak tree,
Regal, sprawling
your body the trunk, strong
roots running deep into the ground, soundly.
Those fingers are also like the tributaries of the Nile Delta,
transporting my blood through my veins to keep my heart beating.

You are a masterpiece
and I am astounded
that you have been exhibited in my world to appreciate,
but if only for a limited amount of time.

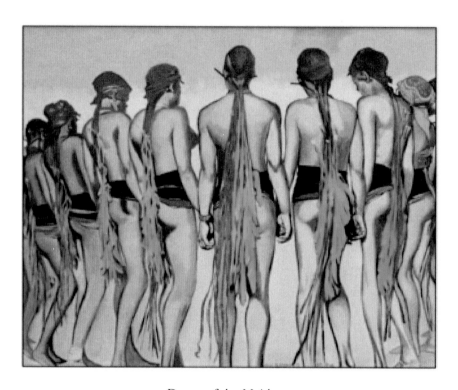

Dance of the Maidens

You Make Me

You make me,
sing
You make me,
dance
You make me,
cry
You make me,
angry
You make me want to write poetry.
You make me,
scream
You make me,
dream
You make me,
sweat
You make me tremble with pleasure when I think of you.
You make me,
happy
You make me,
sad
You make me,
smile,
You make me,
curious
You make me want to look at life through your lens.
You make me,
insatiable
You make me,
crazy
You make me want to change my last name to yours.
You make me,
talk
You make me,
silent
You make me,
listen

You make me,
pray
You make me,
placid
You make me,
blush
You make me,
play
You make me want to run and hide from you.
You make me,
confused
You make me,
question,
You make me,
love
You make me,
You make me,
You make me....

Meanwhile

Two people
Meet
Connect
Talk
Embrace
It feels familiar to them
They step away from it for a while

Then, they come back around full circle
Meeting again
Reconnecting
Holding hands
Kissing

Blissful
Spicy
Roasty
Toasty
Comfortable
Nice

They read between each other's lines
Luscious agitation beginning
'cause the coals are scorching
And the fire is blazing

Hot, verbal liquid is oozing from his lips
Trying to quench her unreachable passion
(*She's so thirsty*)
for more of his burn
so she drinks up as much as she can to put out her inferno
He continues to give her his magic potion from his beautiful mind
until she is satisfied
for now....

Mind Games, Seven Years Times Two

She:
Am I hearing things?
Or, is that really you calling my name?

That sway in your voice.
That, that sweet rhythm of your speech.
That, that flirtation of your tongue,
Emotions running oh so deep.

I fall back seven years times two to a young time in my life.
A time when I was becoming a woman.
Then came you.

The tenderness of your demeanor.
The, the silence of your thunder.
The, the power of your nontouch,
Were all so sexy to me.

How have you been, my dear?

Your game was so intense,
For it was one only you knew how to play.
You held all the pieces, all the rules,
And I fell captive to your way.

What was it about me that made you so crazy?
You would seemingly look right through me.

You saw my very soul.
You, you could read my very thoughts.
You, you would serenade me with your poetic desires,
I was lost in your words.

I couldn't wait until the next time we were together,
Sustained only by my dreams.

You had me so intellectually twisted,
That sometimes, I could not even speak.

What was it about me that made you so crazy?
For you were so much older than I.

He:
You don't understand, my dear.

It was the innocence of your years.
It, it was the naïveness of your view.
It, it was the challenge of your defiance,
The beauty of being you.

Are you ready for me now?
For you are much older, and wiser.
I have since found no one,
Who could quench all of my desires.

She:
Yes I am ready now,
But darling, it is not our time.
For I have since found someone else to play with,
Only this time, this game is mine.

Young Man

Do you realize how many years I am your senior,
young man?
You sure is fine, but I'm old enough to be,
your oldest sister, maybe?

Didn't you hear me?
I'm way too old for you.
But damn, you sure is fine.
No, I can't even go there.
Well, maybe just a lunch, or two.
Meet you where? When?
Okay, I'll see you then.

Our lunch was a very pleasant surprise to me.
Filled with lots of easy laughter and,
ha, good adult conversation.
But then, my stomach started to turn when you said that you wanted to see
me again,
for lunch that is.
I thought that I was off the hook by having lunch with you just once,
but when I looked at you, I knew that it had to be at least that two that I
mentioned,
about ten lines up.

When I got ready to meet you for the second time,
I noticed that my,
heart was beating a little bit faster,
and my,
breathing got just a little bit heavier,
and my,
head got just a tad bit lighter,
and my,
blood started to run slightly warmer,
and my,
brassiere got somewhat tighter,

and my,
uh-oh.
I am truly losing my cool.

As I approached the restaurant that you picked,
I almost turned my car around to drive in the opposite direction,
but, there was a force greater than I that did not allow that to happen.

When we sat down and started talking for a second time,
unmistakable chemistry was also accompanying us for lunch that day.
When your knee brushed against mine, seemingly by accident, it was over for
me then.
I knew that I had to have you.
But I also knew that I had to be careful not to scare you away.

And, and so I,
looked you right in those beautiful, soft brown eyes of yours,
and then I,
melted when you flashed me your perfect, pearly whites,
and then I,
reached for your firm hand and wove your fingers into mine,
and next I,
softly whispered to you,
that I,
found you to be so sweet and so kind,
and then I,
told you that I wanted you,
and that maybe it was fine that you were so much younger than I.

But then I,
said that it was really wrong for us to be here like this,
and that I,
knew we just had to walk away from this,
but it was,
okay for us to feel like this,
because we are only human.

And then we,
both took a moment to pause and think about it and agreed that yes,
we would be just friends.

A Melody to Shirley Bassey

Unexpected

I want to experience what it would be like to be with you.
I want you to hold me in your arms,
and nibble on my ear like I like.
I want to weave my fingers into yours and feel secure.
I want you to find out what makes me, what makes me tick.

I want to be delighted by your desire to peel back the many layers that you say,
hide me so well,
to expose who I really am.

But you already seem to know me,
because you told me exactly what I was thinking.
How did you know?

My head is spinning 'cause *this* was unexpected.
Didn't know this powerful, beautiful chemistry was mu-tu-al.
I think you should go now.
This ain't no good for neither one of us.

The Sweet Wonderment of You

What, what is this?
What *is* this?
You handle my body with such familiarity and care, as if you have been here before.
How did you know that when you kissed me there, that would happen?
And, and how did you know that when you massaged my back like that,
I would respond to you by becoming putty?

Now, how the hell did you know that kissing me ever so slightly,
in that exact spot,
would give you that type of reaction?
Dígame, por favor, Papi (*Tell me please, Daddy.*).
I want to know how many times you have replayed this scenario in your mind.
Or do I really?

Our bodies fused together so perfectly under the glow of the moonlight,
and it was so pretty.
This intersection of mind, body, and soul bears the responsibility of not being charged to coincidence or sheer luck, but to being meant to happen.

I am engulfed by such a feeling of perfect pleasure and a heavy heart at the same time.
Why?
Because,
of the uncertainty of everything.

What an amazing moment in time, interrupting the repetitive rhythm of normalcy.

Now?

(sigh)
This was completely unexpected
But we both knew it was coming
Pent up emotions ready to rupture at any given time
Finally released
Our emotions, raw
It's fire, baby
What is going on? What is happening here?
You want me to listen to you, but I don't want to
Not ready
Not ready to confront what I know is for me
Mine
Assigned
How is it that when we think we have our lives all figured out,
We find out that we don't?
Emotional conflict
What is this that we are both feeling?
Not quite certain how to decipher the plethora of emotions inside of me
Simultaneously vying for first place
I'm not quite ready to pick one of them and say "and the winner is...."
No, not yet
Right now, I am going to safely stay in suspended animation, at least temporarily, insane.
But you seem to complete me....

Sheba Arrives in Jerusalem

Sweet Nothings

I should have known better than to allow you to enter my space, letting you in,
But you were so convincing.
Didn't hurt that you also happened to be pleasing to the eye.
Both your words and inflections harmonized right on cue,
singing sweet nothings in my ear in the perfect key.
After that first performance, all I could hear was your song playing.
You certainly do have the art of charm down to a science, I would say.

How could I be so stupid?
You fooled me, which is quite a feat I might add.
We seemed to be on a journey,
the type of journey that was deep and spiritual,
not at all nomadic, no, but purposeful and unexplainable to others,
that type that only comes around once in a lifetime.

I thought that we were connected by a force greater than both of us
that would propel us from a place of emotional incommodiousness,
to a place of light.
But it appears I was sadly mistaken.

You are so full of fallacy saying you were done with her.
No, you're not.
Found out she's still in your life, right?
Shhhhhhh, hush, darling. You don't owe me any explanation,
for causing me dismay.
No, no, it's okay, really.
I will just quietly fade away from your life
as I play your song, "Sweet nothings."

Discrepancy

Excuse me, Sir, but there seems to be some type of discrepancy here.
You still get so jealous, and that's not cute,
No, not really.

And when I say that I will be your wife,
you run from me like you're going for the gold
and it's so old.

But you have such a hold on me.
All of those years,
tears,
and then quiet resolve.

Making plans to have babies and grow old together—
Is all of that talk just a sick plot to keep me for yourself,
on a shelf?
No, not no museum.

I thought that you loved me,
but there seems to be some type of discrepancy.
Wanna take me to the parade, on your arm for all to see?
No, not no sideshow starting in five, four, three, two...none.

The irritation I feel for you is so incredible, it's borderline hate.
Is it too much to ask of you to deal with your stupid insecurities that you hide behind,
when it's time to commit to me, exclusively?

Can't believe that I finally got the nerve to give you an ultimatum,
to either make it official, or release me.
Finally.

A Reason

Since you have come into my life,
Been trying to find a reason,
but I can't.
And every time that I try to tell you that you have to leave here,
I don't.
What am I gonna do?

You do so many things to me....

You stun me with your flawlessness.
You refresh me with your charm.
You delight me with your touch.
You send me to heights that I have only imagined.

You melt me with your smile.
You turn me on with your style.
And you look right through me with your beautiful, brown eyes.

Your tenderness makes me weak.
You write poetry every time you speak.
You seem to read my every thought,
and make my sentences complete.

Charmed? For sure.
You, my dear, are a sight to behold.
An angel sent down from above,
to shine your rays of light on me to give me joy,
and peace.

By way of chance, we met,
and some kind of magic happened then.
My mind now has a mind of its own,
wandering to places forbidden,
finding succulent, sweet passion that encompasses every single ounce of my being,
catching me up in your rapture.

I should try to stop this thing that is happening between us,
But I won't.
How did I get to this place so suddenly, blinding me?
I'm losing my mind,
trying to find a reason.

My Muse

The brilliance of tonight's full moon against the dark sky has created a senti-
mental mood for me, setting the perfect backdrop for this poetic release....

Life has been so very kind to you,
at least as it appears on your exterior.
I don't even know where to start,
where to begin.

The familiarity of your conversations is causing me to do a double-take,
at my current space and time.
How did this happen? Why?

Your perfect thoughts.
Your perfect words.
You hold the door open for me with the way you build your sentences,
your inflection, your silence.
Funny, I have not even had the pleasure of seeing you yet,
and this is the case.

I dare not think about our first encounter, face-to-face,
after what really is a lifetime since I have seen you,
in your skin.

When we speak, revealing our thoughts, we realize that we,
simultaneously,
have been pondering the exact, same, things.
What a feeling of excitement this creates,
but with such emotional responsibility on its heels.

Do I?
Do we,
explore the possibilities
of running away together at this point in time?
Do we,
attempt to figuratively turn back the hands of time to do what we both have imagined

more than one time too many,
to find out if it is really true,
this emotional blaze whose fire can only be put out by you,
by responding to my 911 plea?

My muse, my muse....

The Valentine in My Mind

The first time that I saw you,
there was a feeling inside of me.
A feeling indescribable,
a feeling I could not reach.

I needed time to think it over,
to see if this feeling was really true.
I told you I was ready to open up,
I had to be with only you.

Then, you said you didn't understand me.
I often asked myself, "Why?"
My mind told me not to worry,
but the heart never tells a lie.

It was true, I had the chance,
however, I played with time
Now all that you could ever be to me,
is the valentine in my mind.

She

She hurt you again, didn't she?
She made you cry again, right?
She made you question your swagger, your sex appeal, your effect.

She caused a scene,
making it seem,
like it was you again, am I correct?

Another day turned sour before it began?
Another evening watching the clock, then the door, then it's 2:00 am.
What happened to dinner for two?

Next day, more of the same, mundane.
Aren't you tired of the same song whose hook has been a panacea to mask the
lies to get you through to the next?

How long has it been since she's been with you only?
You gotta be lonely.
Why are you putting up with this?
I'm sick of hearing about this, this sick game she is playing with you.
Aren't you too?

If she were me, then there would be no more pain,
no more anger, no more shame.
If I were she, you and your sheets would have company every evening,
like the clock that you have been watching.

Tick, tock.

The sands of time have run down, very low.
But can't you see, you can flip the hourglass over and start fresh,
with me.

If you do, then she will be me.

If By Chance

I refuse to speak your name again,
because if I do,
it would mean that I acknowledge that you are still in my blood.

I won't dwell on the image of you that pops into my mind,
because if that happens,
a permanent photo will forever remain there.

I will not ponder on our impromptu dinners,
when we would spend hours,
fantasizing about a future that we would never share.

I quickly perish the thought,
like the sudden change of the wind in March,
of seeing you again,
but if only for one second.
Because I know it would become,
another cloud of false hope and sweet pain, hovering over me.
Damn you, for me falling in love with you,
a perfectly flawed dream.

And if by chance I do see you again,
let's just share a simple kiss, say "good-bye,"
and then go our separate ways.

Gone Forever

It started years ago.
The childish games I would play with you.
But you were serious.
You really cared.
I took you for granted.
Oh, you'll always be there.

Enough was enough.
Your feelings had been hurt for the last time.
So you went away.

Then, when I realized what I had lost,
I went after you.
But it was too late.
Because you were gone forever.

The Tide

While standing on this beach of white sand,
I can see the tide coming for you on the horizon.

I knew our time together was just for a season,
But I didn't know it would be ending this soon.

I'd hope that we'd have just one more time to climb these here mountains together.
I'd thought we could sit by an evening fire and get lost in the darkness that would engulf us,
Just one more time.

What about our endless walks on this here beach, hand in hand?
I ache thinking about the colors of the morning we will no longer see together,
As night makes way for day, like clockwork.

Oh, dear, the tide has come.
Good-bye, my sweet.

Rain

Woke up around five-thirty this
morning,

and I was sad.

Is it raining?

No.

Must be you then,

getting ready to break my heart.

Almost

We would think the same thoughts at the same time,
feel the same things
from hundreds of miles away.
We were of one heart, one mind.
Synchronized.

You would tell me when I felt distant from you,
while from afar.
How did you know that I was struggling with my feelings for you,
all the way from there?

You seemed to be so ready to make a new path into tomorrow,
not knowing where it would lead and you wanted me to go with you.
But I hesitated because I was scared.
Wasn't quite ready.
And you couldn't wait for me to make up my mind.
I understand.

Now, you have completely disappeared from my life, like a vapor.
No trace of you and I am so heartbroken.
I am aching to reach out to you,
to hear you speak my name.
I will never know this type of love again.
Never.

You are really gone now, bowing out so gracefully.
I know you couldn't stay suspended forever, waiting for me.

Almost, almost....

Chapter Three
Reflections from the Mirror of Life

Glancing at a mirror can be quite difficult at times,
but most of the time,
it does not lie to us,
shattering what we believe our truths are.

We sometimes just need a quiet space,
giving us the solitude necessary,
to hear that still, small voice,
and to really see and understand,
what our reflection shows us.

To assess who we are,
we must look directly into this mirror of life,
and confront ourselves and embrace who we see,
looking right back at us.

We have to take the time to reflect
on everything in our lives,
past and present and on the possibilities of tomorrow,
the joy, the pain, and the indifference,
to realize that we have all of the tools that we need,
to continue on our respective journeys.

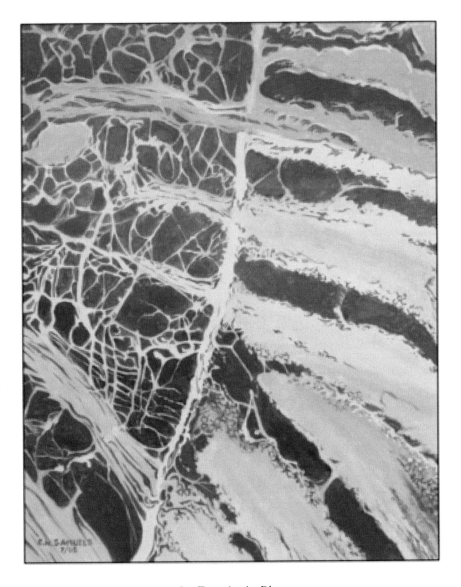

An Exercise in Blue

Reflections

To know where we are going,
and to truly enjoy present blessings,
we must take a moment to glance backwards at the road behind us,
to appreciate our current place in life.

Sometimes, this is not an easy task,
because we might just see a period, question mark or comma,
that we would like to go back and change in our life's story.

However, our history is something that we can never erase,
so, we must try to continue on the journey that our pen and paper is taking us
on,
and continue to write.

That old cliché "Hindsight is twenty-twenty" is so true.
But, what we have is an unknown quest forward.

So, dare to seize today.
It might be tomorrow, soon enough.

Sunday Evening

Though you were in my life for just a brief time,
you made such a profound impact on my entire being.

The connection was so strong between us,
my heart would ache sometimes when I didn't get to see or talk to you.

Vivid, colorful visions of you now dance in my head,
beginning and ending as though I were watching a favorite show.

Even though you are no longer here on this earth,
I still have thoughts of you that creep into my mind often,
like a thief in the night.

I do not know exactly what it is about a Sunday evening,
that makes me think of you.

I have been standing outside for a while now,
and this comfortable air is making me really sentimental,
calling up thoughts of yesteryear, of things that were familiar to us.
Why did you have to go so soon?

It's getting dark now and I must go inside.
As the tears roll down my face, I smile as I think to myself,
I'll see you again on another Sunday evening.

Just Let Me Be

There are things that I have to deal with, alone.
So let me be.

Sometimes I feel lost, lonely and mad at myself.
So please, just let me be.

No, I don't want your kind words, thoughts, or sympathy.
Just go and let me be!

Can't you understand? I must tread this road alone!
So go away, and let me be.

Yes, it is hard at times to face and overcome obstacles successfully.
Even so, just let me be.

Time is the only friend who can help me now.
So just go and let me be.

Maybe someday, you will accompany me.
But for now, my friend, just go and let me be.

There I Go

There I go, singing that same ol' song again.
But you never listen to it,
Though you say you do.
Nothing matters to you.

From day to day,
You have no direction, no path.
Why don't I just leave you be?
You cause me nothing, nothing but frustration, anguish, and pain!

Pitter patter, pitter patter.
Look, here comes the rain.
Once more, it's synonymous with my pain.

Don't you see? You're just wasting away.
I know. I know! There I go.
Singing that same ol' song, once again.

What If?

What if there were no music?
What if there were no dance?
What if there were no color?
Just the thought I could not stand.

What if there were no sax, trombone, or harp,
To serenade us in the park?
There would be no classical music, jazz, or hip hop,
To make us sway, snap, and rock.

What if there were no stage,
To bring a written script to life?
What if there were no crayons,
In which little ones find delight?

What if there were no place,
For us to browse and see?
The works of many artists,
Creating their part of history.

What if there were no one,
Who dared to share their gift?
What if there were no poetry,
Where euphoria can truly exist?

Oh, but thank goodness we do have art!
In many forms that banish strife.
Let's savor its awesome brilliance then,
Of royal gifts transcending life.

Sean Dalton

As an infant, I watched you play in the evening,
and I was overjoyed at the discoveries that you were so pleased with.
I smiled because my heart was warmed by the gift that each memory which was created,
left behind at the close of another day.

As a toddler, in the afternoon, we would walk with the bright sun behind us,
and I was touched by your little shadow next to mine.
I would look down at you and smile,
and you would look up at me and smile back.

Next, I realized that I was out of breath,
because all of a sudden, we started to run,
to see a group of ducks by the banks of the lake.

Then, we would take our time,
and work our way around,
the entire circumference of that lake,
neither of us ready to leave for different reasons.
Yours, for reasons of exploration.
Mine, because I wanted to let each and every moment we spent together,
linger.

Soon enough, I know that you will grow into a wonderful, young man.
and my son will not be a little boy anymore.
And one day, you will leave the nest to create your own story.
So for now, I will savor as much time as I can,
while your footprints are still small.

34th Street between Broadway and Seventh Avenue in Manhattan

Beautiful, elegant, and delicate.
You don't walk, you glide.

Seasoned, graceful, and poised.
Your salt and pepper hair reveals your wisdom.

Radiant, glowing, and happy.
Your electric smile is contagious.

Sexy, funky, spunky and fly.
Girl, do you realize that you still got it going on?

Do you remember how I used to emulate you as a little girl?
Painting my fingers and toes, trying on your pearls?
Awkwardly walking in your heels?
Putting on your makeup, red lipstick, and your hair?

As I got older, do you recall how I would try to walk like you,
talk like you, and sound like you,
with your calming tone that can bring peace and still to the most chaotic of situations?

As the years continued to roll by, do you also remember that scene
on 34th Street between Broadway and Seventh Avenue as a teen?
I thought I was fly then and had it going on.
But on that crowded street, you checked me,
with a backhand to my mouth,
that stung like an inoculation, and I was so angry.
However, you did not even flinch one bit, said that the day was done,
and in silence, we headed for the iron horse, going uptown on the number
one.

As you can see, that day is forever embedded in my mind,
crystal-clear, as if it happened yesterday.
I would call it a turning point in my life, realizing how precious you were.

Then, you became my friend.
Then, we started to have cups of hot tea together
and talk for hours. And now, we still do.

Over the years, as a woman, I realized that I have become more like you,
Mom.
People say that I walk like you, talk like you, sound like you, and can bring
peace and still to the most chaotic of situations, too.
And so I thank you.
Thank you for such a beautiful relationship that I will cherish, forever,
my mother and my friend.

Riverside Drive
(Written May 2008)

Such a patient man:
Spending so much time with me as an infant,
Relieving my mother in the evenings when you would come home from a
long day at work.
"Does the baby want some cool water?" you would ask.
"Cool water, nice cool water," I would answer.

Such an intelligent man:
Your avid reading and reciting poetry,
created an environment for my craving of books at a very young age.
And so you read to me.
"Read book, read book," I would say.
You'd smile, tuck me in my bed, and read to me,
your velvety voice lulling me to sleep.

Ahhh, the many memories that were made on Riverside Drive are countless.
But I can reach out and touch many of them,
because they are so vivid and real to me, even now.

The running, the bike riding, the swings, the sandbox, the roller skates, the
scrapes,
the car washing, and then,
just the simple walk.
The simple, slow, meaningful walk down Riverside Drive with you,
as you near three-quarters of a century old,
was priceless.

As we took that walk on that beautiful spring day,
you started to reminisce about the fun times that you had as a youth on
Riverside Drive.
Your descriptions were so incisive, I felt like I was right there with you, during
that time.

But, time has caught up with you and you have not had an easy road to walk.
Your resilience amazes everyone.
You still paint, you still read and recite poetry.
You still laugh, you still smile, you still encourage and admonish,
and you,
still walk down Riverside Drive.

I never could have known,
the significance that one, simple walk,
on a street, where I have probably walked in my same footsteps,
more than a million times, would have on me.

Thank you, Dad, for that slow, simple walk down Riverside Drive.

6:15 PM

Dear Daddy,

You know, I had a feeling that day,
and as I stand here, staring at your picture now,
it is very strange, but it is as if you were still around.
When I am outside now on a brilliant, sunny day,
I can still hear your laughter and see that million-dollar smile.

When I walk outside of my house,
I can still see you peacefully and thoughtfully relaxing in that chair,
when you came to visit us in May,
fully absorbing all of the beauty of what God has created,
as though you knew it would be your last time here.
And it was.

When I call home now,
I only hear Mommy's sweet, familiar voice on the other end of the phone
because you are no longer there.
Yes, you are with God now, resting peacefully in his bosom.

6:15 pm,
you transitioned from this world to a glorious place that we cannot see.
6:15 pm,
the time you answered the call from God, to come on home. To rest forever.
6:15 pm,
the same time, hundreds of miles away from you, I resigned myself to changing
up my routine for that Monday evening, going home to just quietly ponder.
I guess I somehow knew my life would be changed forever at that exact point
in time.

I will miss you sorely, but will fondly remember you forever.
With love that knows no boundaries
your daughter,

Andrea

Dawn Comes to Darfur

Welcome Home

Harlem.

Even though you are being renovated,
as I comfortably ride across town in a yellow cab on 126th Street coming from the airport,
I see the ugly reality of you that still exists in the shadows of what's shiny and new,
of what I saw growing up in the city.

While at a stoplight,
I see a broken woman being beaten down by life and the crack demon,
as her "wonderful" boyfriend screams on her on the crowded sidewalk,
to try to take the attention away from his crack-addicted self, so he thinks.
Then I watch this broken woman run to reach for the handle of a gypsy cab,
as he reaches for it too.

The light changes,
and I sadly watch her as far as I can as the cab moves farther west.
I shake my head and say a prayer for her because there is nothing else that I can do.

Dime Candy and Dill Pickles

Stopped at a gas station this morning on the other side of town
and it had been a long time since I experienced a place like that.
It took me back to a feel-good time,
when you could get a pack of candy for a dime.

They had Now and Laters, one at a time, not by the pack.
Candy and dill pickles galore.
Twinkies, cigarettes, human hair by the pack,
incense, scented body oil, pantyhose that don't fit,
and you could play the lottery too.

Reminded me of Ralph's Variety near 145th and Amsterdam in Hamilton Heights
I think the outside of the store was bright pink? Right?
He had Disco Dish candy (remember that?) and Big Bol gum!

Reminded me of Willie Burger,
that used to be on the corner of Frederick Douglass Boulevard and 145th in
Harlem.
Yum!

Reminded me of me and my girls posing like we were fly for Polaroid photo-
graphs on 42nd Street
before the city cleaned it up.

Reminded me of me going down to Delancey Street to get my sheepskin.

Reminded me of the days when it was cool to jump in the pool with our Nikes on,
and of my first Louis Vuitton and Gucci bags that I had.

Dime candy and dill pickles.

Reminded me of,
Leng Fong's on Broadway near 145th .
Dag, that was some of the best Chinese food!

Reminded me of Fordham Road in the Boogie Down, where we would get
our sweat suits for field day,
with our nick names and zodiac signs on them. What?

Reminded me when I would ask my friends,
Valerie and Lisa, to teach me cuss words in Spanish,
much to my parents' chagrin.

Reminded me of the yellow and green Italian icy days,
when we would flip it over and scrape the bottom,
lips and tongue red from the cherry dye.

Reminded me of cherry fights on the back of the A train after school.

Dime candy and dill pickles.

I miss those carefree days when life seemed a whole lot simpler.

Oh, yes! I'm sorry, Sir. May I please have twenty on pump ten?

The Great Door of Time

The years go by.
I look back on those memories.
Memories captured in my mind.
How quickly I have grown.
It's sad to me sometimes to see,
How I've grown and reached maturity.
The happy times,
The sad.
O, I wish I could step back,
step back through the door.
The great door of time...

The late Calvin H. Samuels

About the Author

Andrea Lynn Samuels came across quite a few old programs from the early seventies and realized that she had been reciting poetry since the age of four. She has taken some of the poetry that she has secretly written over the span of thirty years, and has honored the memory of her beloved dad, cancer warrior Calvin H. Samuels, by weaving some of his paintings into her book. Calvin painted most of the paintings in this book while he fiercely battled cancer. Shortly after her father's passing, Andrea's mother, Lottie G. Samuels, charged her with continuing to carry the torch, passed to her by  her dad, which was a much needed push, as she hesitated to follow through on publishing this book.

Andrea has also given back to help others through her participation in numerous fundraising drives and events, as well as giving her time through volunteerism. She is also honoring her father's memory by donating a portion of the proceeds from her book to the Calvin H. Samuels Memorial Fund for cancer research, created by the Development Department at St. Luke's Roosevelt Hospital in New York City, where her dad received superb care as well as other organizations that are fighting the disease.

Andrea was born and raised in New York, New York (Manhattan). She attended and graduated from A. Philip Randolph Campus High School in Manhattan, which happened to be the old High School of Music and Art building where her dad graduated from many years before Andrea was but a speck. The school then became the Fiorello H. LaGuardia High School of Music and Art, now located at Lincoln Center. She is an alumnus of

South Carolina State University in Orangeburg, South Carolina, where she majored in Marketing. She has one son who she greatly admires and resides in Charlotte, North Carolina.

www.andreawrites.org